Hate Love and Loneliness

Jose Aguillon Jr

iUniverse, Inc.
New York Bloomington

Hate Love and Loneliness

iUniverse books may be ordered through booksellers or by contacting:

iUniverse
1663 Liberty Drive
Bloomington, IN 47403
www.iuniverse.com
1-800-Authors (1-800-288-4677)

ISBN: 978-1-4401-2064-0 (pbk)
ISBN: 978-1-4401-3398-5 (ebk)

Printed in the United States of America

iUniverse rev. date: 3/19/2009

Another

Another day has gone by,
Another tear has been shed,
Another heart has been broken,
Another life has been taken,
Another person has walked by,
Another leaf has fallen from the tree,
Another bird has left its nest,
Another women has given birth,
Another child has been beaten,
Another sin has been committed,
Another sad soul is depressed,
Another teenager wants to kill themselves,
Another dream has come true,
Another gun has been shot,
Another thought has ran through my mind,
And another life has been taken.

Jose Aguillon Jr

Where are you?

You'll never understand me, but that's okay. You were still proud of me no matter what. Helped me when I needed it, and took care of me when I was a
Child. All that time I always wondered where my father was? What does he look like? Like me? Is he outgoing? I don't think he even cares. In the twenty-two years he hasn't called or written. Does he want to meet me? Does he even care about me? The only thing I have in common is drinking, but I would never leave my seed behind. I would never run like a coward. I will suffer the rain and pain. Face the struggle, just to make my child happy. Teach him right from wrong. Not to do all the bad things I have done, but to learn from my mistakes. Always be yourself and never take anything for granted. Treat a woman the way she is suppose to be treated. Never to disrespect her or lift a hand. But only in offer your hand in marriage. And most important never to run away like my father did from me.

Jose Aguillon Jr

Cause

Can't go to sleep cause I'm sober,
Can't eat cause I'm nervous,
Can't smile cause I'm not happy,
Can't see cause it's dark,
Can't fly cause I have no wings,
Can't escape cause I'm not free,
Can't love again cause my heart is broken,
Can't cry cause I have no more tears left,
Can't feel whole cause I'm alone,
Can't shine cause I'm not a star,
Can't breath cause your not here,
Can't be found cause I'm lost,
Can't die cause I'm already dead.

Jose Aguillon Jr

Of

I'm tired of being rejected,
I'm tired of dirty looks,
I'm tired of being alone,
I'm tired of shedding tears,
I'm tired of not being at that level,
I'm tired of myself,
I'm tired of depression,
I'm tired of getting judged,
I'm tired of life,
I'm tired of missing my relatives,
I'm tired of seeing my family struggle,
I'm tired of not having inspiration,
I'm tired of writer's block,
I'm tired of making mistakes,
I'm still tired and always will be,
I will die tired.

Jose Aguillon Jr

The reason

Give me a reason to live,
Give me a reason to go on,
Give me a reason to smile,
Give me a reason not to cry,
Give me a reason to love,
Give me a reason to trust,
Please give me a reason.

The Season

The spring can be cold but sometimes warm,
When summer comes it can be very hot, but it can
Also rain,
In fall everything starts to change colors and leaves start to fall
from the trees,
Winter finally comes and it gets cold and snow starts to fall,
Sometimes we don't want the seasons to change, but
The cycle must go on.

Jose Aguillon Jr

The Perfect Rose

I start to look for,
Not too tall,
And not short,
With a little bit of color,
Bloom,
Just growing,
Soaking the water,
Taking in the sun,
Moving left to right,
From the light breeze,
Then I saw it,
Standing still,
Dark red,
No thorns on the steam,
As I take a step,
Reach out with my arm,
To touch you,
Then the gardener grabs you and takes you away from me.

The Real me

Starting to think,
Then I blink,
And start to see,
What I pretend to be,
Someone else,
Not myself,
Since I hate it,
But I fake it,
I am Jose
So I pray,
For the strength,
I start to hold my breath,
Hoping my heart would stop,
Never reaching to the top,
All of a sudden I fall,
Get up and walking through an empty hall,
Feeling so lost,
At what cost,
Would I go,
Just to show,
The real person,
That I am.

Jose Aguillon Jr

Judgment

I can stand my life,
That I try to live,
But I can t,
Stand this stress,
That you but on me,
I try to be the best person that I can be,
I can't satisfy,
Everybody,
So if you don't,
Like the person that I am,
Don't judge me,
Cause I try to be,
Like you,
Because if I didn't,
You would,
Hate me.

Jose Aguillon Jr

The Truth

Words that I think,
That I start to write,
What comes from my Heart,
My inner feelings,
That I can express,
When you read,
These touching words,
You can tell how I felt,
Then understand,
What I say is true,
And not a lie.

Jose Aguillon Jr

The start

The sun starts to set and stars start to shine.
Leaves start to grow in spring and start falling in fall.
Rain turns into snow and water turns into ice.
Happiness turns into sadness and frowns turn into sorrow.
Life starts to hurt and with time the pain goes away.
Memories start to fade away and then forget the past.
Hair turns gray and skin turns into wrinkles.
Light turns in to darkness and fear turns loose.
A heart starts to heal and another one is broken.
Another smile starts to appear and another tear begins to fall.
Birth turns into death and funerals turn into gatherings.
Water turns to wine and man turns evil.

Jose Aguillon Jr

You

Why is it every time you walk by, I can't keep my eyes off of you. Then my heart stops beating and when I can't see you anymore it begins to beat again. Funny feelings inside I get. You are so beautiful in so many ways. If you were mine I would never stop saying I love you. Running my fingers through your hair. Looking into your eyes and getting lost in another world. But when I see you looking at me. It will never be. I guess the only thing I can do is dream and cry of sadness.

Jose Aguillon Jr

Only One Person

Words and thoughts running in my mind,
Good and evil,
But I can't help it,
Making mistakes and bad choices,
Is a part of life,
With tears falling from pity,
Walking with my head down,
Feeling so alone,
Ask me what's wrong,
But I won't say,
What I really want,
Keeping it all inside,
Only for me to know,
And nobody else,

Jose Aguillon Jr

Time

A time to love,
And a time to feel pain,
A time to live,
And a time to die,
A time for fun,
And a time for work,
A time to be Happy,
And a time to be sad,
A time for bleeding,
And a time for healing,
A time for young age,
And a time of old age,
A time for birth,
And a time for death,
A time to shine,
And a time to rain,
A time to crawl,
And a time to walk,
A time to say hello,
And a time to say goodbye.

Jose Aguillon Jr

Being alone

An angel from above,
When it came to our love,
You were one of a kind,
Never listening to your mind,
And always your heart,
Trying to keep us from falling apart,
Trying to be together,
You said it would last forever,
Words could never express,
All the times I was depressed,
Spending nights in the dark,
With lonely walks in the park,
Tear after tear,
Being without you was my only fear,
Not holding you in my arms,
Keeping me from harm,
Only from myself,
And nobody else,
Things will never be the same,
I have only myself to blame,
For letting you go,
Now I have nothing to show,
For all these years,
Except for falling tears.

Jose Aguillon Jr

Goodbye

I have to say it,
But I don't want to,
Please don't leave,
From my sight,
Just stay one more time,
Please don't leave me,
Here all alone,
With nobody to talk to,
But myself,
To vent all my feelings,
And not keep them inside,
You say you have to leave,
But do you really have to,
I guess I can't keep you back,
So I guess we have to go our own ways,
And now it's time to say what I don't want to,
Goodbye.

Jose Aguillon Jr

Trying

Something to say,
But don't know how,
Trying to breath,
But there's no air,
Trying to live,
But I'm lost in life,
Finding the right path,
But don't know where to walk,
Opening my eyes,
But I can't see,
Trying to feel,
But I can't touch,
Trying to love,
But I can't trust again,
Trying to write,
But I don't know what too,
Trying to remember,
But I can't,
Trying to smile,
But I'm not happy,
Trying is the only thing that I can do,
And so can you.

Jose Aguillon Jr

Dreaming

To dream of what you want in life
Being successful
Having that special someone
Hating the bad dreams
Where you can see your own death
To see myself at an old age
A dream that confuses you
To keep me pondering when I wake up
Wanting to lay down and fall asleep
So I can finally get away from all this
With only one more dream

Jose Aguillon Jr

True feelings

I can't stop thinking of you
How is this
Please get these thoughts out of my head
I won't tell you how I truly feel
Only being afraid that you will hurt me
And leave me
Avoiding the pain
That I would have to feel
So understand, why I don't tell you
Things have happened in the past
So don't take it personal

Jose Aguillon Jr

Inside

Trying to keep my head up
But it's stuck in the ground
So no one can see
The expressions
Keeping my feelings in this hole
Waiting for them escape
Trying to find its way out
Hurting for months
When one day I explode
From all the anger
Hating the aftermath
Apologizing for my actions
Wishing it would never happen
But these things need to come out
No matter how much you hide them

Jose Aguillon Jr

With you

When I'm with you
I feel so happy
How can this be?
Those eyes and hips
Looking so good
Not caring what anybody else thinks
Making me feel humble and at peace
The way you say those words
Letting me know how you feel
Keep writing what you want
Don't care what other people say
And be yourself
Cause that's what make you special

Jose Aguillon Jr

Dead

They call me dead
Lying in my coffin
Is where I can see myself
When my spirit rises
To see everyone
With falling tears from my family
Feeling sad to see them in pain
Why was I taken away?
Wishing I could of done so much
But now I sit in these clouds
Watching you from above
Knowing I will always be by your side

Jose Aguillon jr

EASY TO HARD

Easy to say yes
Hard to say no
Saying hello is easy
Saying goodbye is hard
Dying is easy
Living is hard
Not to some one love is easy
To love some is hard
Hearing is easy
Listening is hard
Closing my eyes is easy
Opening my eyes is hard
Easy to tell a lie
Hard to tell the truth

Jose Aguillon Jr

You Know Who

I want touch you
but I can't
You already know
What we can't do
My mind is in a million places
I am so lost
But you make me feel safe
You are my shelter
For my rainy days
The one I can talk too
Being alone
Is what I really need
At this point of my life
I am so thankful
That I got to meet you

Jose Aguillon Jr

The Sky

A clould in the sky
Flying so freely
Moving slow
Seeing many places
More cloulds start to come
Darkness covers the sky
Thunder is loud
Winds start blowing
And it finally starts pouring out

Piece

One day soon
The pieces of the puzzle
Will come together
They might be missing
But you have to look hard
And one day
You will find the missing piece
The time spent will make it worth it

Fly

Free as a bird
My wings are healed
I can fly anywhere
Going many places
That I used to go
I'm back home
Here to stay
Ready for the world
So I spread my wings open
And fly away

Don't Love

I don't believe in love
Not anymore
You tore me apart
Brought me into tears
Put a crack in my heart
Made it hard to breathe
Cupid don't shoot me
With your love arrow
Refusing you
Alone is where I'll be
So please don't find me again

Will

Will I fall
Will I rise
Where will I go
Where will I end up
Will I shine like a star
Will you feel what I say
Or will you not understand
The complex messages
I try to explain
Read between the lines
And find what it means

Without you

I can finally breathe
Without you
I can finally fly
Without you
I can finally speak
Without you
I can finally see
Without you
I can finally taste life
Without you
I can finally be happy
Without you
I can finally be myself
Without you
I can finally be free

The Movie

Life isn't like a movie
But I wish it was
My happy ending
That I never had
I could be someone else
For only one moment
A hero
A handsome man
A perfect man
A person I couldn't be
In real life

My True Love

You get me through the day
You get me through the night
Looking forward to hearing you
Singing those beautiful words
The wonderful beat
That I nod my head too
You got me through rough times
You got me through the happy times
A smile on my face
A frown on my face
Thank you for always being there for me
You will never understand
How much I depend on you
You're my only love
Sorry I pushed you away
But I came back
Now I am ready to make you
And write you
With a final product which is a song
Is the only way I can pay you back
So I can touch someone
Like you touched me

My Special Someone

Let me give you a kiss
Tell me if you like it
Was it everything you wanted
Do you regret it
I've been waiting
For this moment for so long
You have been in my mind
For quite some time
Only if you knew
What my thoughts are
Let me take you out to eat
Pull out your chair
And wispher something sweet
Into your ear
Ask you too slow dance
You'll look into my eyes
Then you can see
How much you mean to me

My Choice

How could this be
Can this be real
I'm with someone else
But I can't keep you
Out of my mind
What should I do
Maybe I'll leave her
So I could be with you
Will I make the right choice
Trying to fallow my heart
And not my mind
Which one will I choose

They're for you

You cry at night
But I'll wake up
And take care of you
Holding you
Until you stop crying
Rock you to sleep
Give you a kiss good night
Letting you go
On the first day of school
Watching you grow everyday
Teaching you right from wrong
Always say thank you and your welcome
Respecting mother and father
I'll always love you no matter what
Know I will always be there for you
When you finally get married
I know you will do the same
For your child

U~s~

You knew I was doing wrong
But you didn't say anything
Sorry I let you down
I'm trying to make it right
Never calling you
Missing your birthday
You gave me money
When you shouldn't have
Why did you
I know you couldn't give us much
Your love was the only thing we needed
Thank you for everything you did
You had two roles
Mom and dad
Life was hard
But you kept us together
What would I do without you
Miles and miles away
A phone call is all it takes
For me to tell you I love you
I miss you
Can't wait to see you

Leaving

Leaving so I can be alone
Leaving so I can be drama free
Leaving so I can be without you
Leaving so I can make it
Leaving so I can be set free
Leaving so I can grow
Leaving so I can be myself
Leaving so I can feel life
Leaving so I can be happy
Leaving so I can plan
Leaving so I can be on my own
Leaving was the best choice I ever made
Leaving is always hard but just give it time
Leaving will never be easy
Leaving maybe the only choice you have

Trust

Trust no more
I won't let anyone
Come back inside
My door is closed
No way out
Feelings are stuck
Locked away
For my thoughts only
You make me not believe
In trusting again
Words you said
Actions that were made
That make me not trust
A soul on this earth

Woman of my Dreams

Woman of my Dreams
Doesn't exist
Only finding you
When I sleep
Thinking I found
What I truly wanted
But then I got to know
The real you

Woman of my Dreams
Where can you be
I'm still waiting
To meet you
In real person
Please come to my rescue
Hold me tight
Tell me it's going to be okay

Woman of my Dreams
That doesn't call me names
Who isn't selfish
Won't put me down
Taking my heart
And not breaking it
Keeping all my thoughts
Too yourself

Woman of my Dreams
I will be here
Just come to reality
Make my dreams come true
Prove to me that love still lives
Make me cry tears of happiness
Can you just come true
So I don't have to dream anymore

Blind

Open my eyes
Let me see the truth
How could I be so blind
After all these years
I just let it walk by
Noticing nothing
It was sitting right by me
Invisible to the naked eye
But I figured it out
You only wanted
Things to make you happy
No matter how you got it
Even if it made you miserable
Didn't want to let go
Now I am gone
So quick to jump
To another relationship
Let's me really know
That you never loved me
And it hurts
Because I spent time
Away from
Family and friends
Making up for lost time
Is all I have to do
You wanted to hold me down
I'm coming up now
So I can fly away

Doesn't

Sorry doesn't fix it
Sorry doesn't cure it
Sorry doesn't close the wounds
Sorry doesn't stop the bleeding
Sorry doesn't bring back the time
Sorry doesn't stop the hate
Sorry doesn't take the pain
Sorry doesn't make me listen
Sorry doesn't let me care
Sorry doesn't mean a thing to me
So keep your words and thoughts to yourself

Moment

Take a picture
Frozen in time
A moment of happiness
I can look at it
When I am down
Start thinking
About that moment
That brought joy
Into my life
Keep it on my wall
So I can reminisce
When I see it

Sunlight

My sunny day
Is finally here
The storm has passed
Raindrops are drying up
Sunlight gives me hope
Clouds start disappearing
Plants can now make oxygen
So they can grow

Feel

Hold you tight
So I can feel safe
You make me feel
Like I can do anything
Go beyond the skies
Touch the stars
Bring a smile to my face
When I see you walking towards me
Kiss me on the lips
Tell me you missed me
Hold my hand
So they can know were together
Make me feel something
That I have never felt before
I never knew these feelings existed
Until you came into my life

Thoughts of You

I don't want to see your face
Or hear your name
You make me angry
When you cross my mind
Wishing I never met you
Would make me glad
So the thoughts of you
Were never true

Why didn't daddy come home

Why didn't daddy come home
Waiting by the door
Why didn't daddy come home
Looking out the window
Why didn't daddy come home
Teaching myself to shave
Why didn't daddy come home
Mother had to work so hard
Why didn't daddy come home
Brothers had to raise me
Why didn't daddy come home
No food to eat
Why didn't daddy come home
I felt so lonely without you
Why didn't daddy come home
Missing you but I never met you
Why didn't daddy come home
Birthday presents that you never brought me
Why didn't daddy come home
Wondering when you were coming home
But you never did

Hate Love and Loneliness

If you say my words
Aren't meaningful
Then you don't understand
What I have to say
Words that come from
Hate, Love and Loneliness

Only for the Kids

Only for the kids
Was the reason you stayed
Only for the kids
Was the reason you said I love you
Only for the kids
Was the reason I took pictures
Only for the kids
Was the reason I worked so hard
Only for the kids
Was the reason I never left
Only for the kids
Was the reason you kissed me
Only for the kids
Was the reason I never cheated
Only for the kids
Was the reason we have a home
Only for the kids
Is the reason you and I are together

In your Memory

You left so soon
I'll never forget that morning
Word got around what happened
My heart stopped
How can something happen
To such a great person
You were always happy
Never did I see you mad
Can't believe you left
Everything happens for a reason
God wrote our paths
Before we were born
Only he knows
What the future holds for us
Make everyday count
Take advantage of the moment
Don't hold back your feelings
We will always miss you
Hold you in our hearts
Place you in our prayers
It was my honor
Meeting a great person like you

Single

The single life
You say you love it
But you wake up lonely
Wishing I would come back
Knowing thats not going to happen
Hurts you everyday
Choosing to make myself happy
Without you
Puts a smile to my face
People make mistakes
Meeting you was one of them
And Letting you into my heart
Don't let it happen again
Is what I tell myself
Not wanting to fall in love again
Is your fault
How does that feel
Knowing you caused that

Until

Lay in bed until noon
Well look into each others eyes
Blow me a kiss
That I will catch
Tell me that you love me
No matter what happens
Proud to call me yours
You will hug me
Doesn't matter who's around
We will be in our own little world
Laying in bed until noon

All alone

Sitting at the table
All alone
Waiting for you to come
It's been thirty minutes
Still not here
You never called
Where could you be
Looking in my phone book
But you were never added
A thought came to my mind
You aren't real
So I sit here all alone

In your eyes

Hold you in my arms
My lucky charm
Look at me
How could it be
Just want to hold you
I'll stay true
Hold hands in the park
The little spark
In your eye
I can't say bye
Let me know how you feel
What we talk about is real
You won't tell anybody
Let me touch your body
Feeling your skin
Don't know where you have been
Let me into your heart
Don't break us apart
Trying to tell
How I felt
When I am with you
My boo
Give you the key
So you don't flee
After I open up
Then up stump
On the words you want to say
Let's just lay
On this bed
When I let you in my head
What will you think
When you start to blink
Tell me that my hear is pure
Will be sure
When I open the door
That you will still be there

The Song

Remember the song
We use to listen too
When we were together
To feel so special
Being with you
At the special moment
Words that were so beautiful
Touching my heart
Like no one else could
Remember the words
That made us cry
Feeling so loved
By each other
No one could take that away
From two people
Who felt so strong
About one another
Remember that song
Will always be there for both of us
Even when your not with me anymore

Dark

On this dark path I walk
Make sure one foot goes first
Don't trip on the crack
Your eyes will adjust
Too this darkness
That you see every night
Keep walking
You will be there soon
Street lights give hope
So I don't stay blind

Back to her

Don't run
Where do you say
Back to her
Stay away
As far as I can
Never look back
She's not worth it
Running back
I thought it was my only option
Leaving and coming back
This time I'm gone for forever
Good bye to that part of my life
Start a new chapter
With only me in it
Who knows what will happen
But at least I won't run back to her

Only comes once

True love only comes once
If you really believe in it
It will come once
Hold your partner
Wipe away every tear
Get through every fight
That is love, that only comes once
When you wake up in the morning
You know the person laying next to you
Is the most beautiful person in the world
Knowing no one can take that away
From both of you
Is so powerful
So on this day of marriage
You can tell that true love only comes once

What I lost

The smell of you
Still drives me crazy
Can't believe you're gone
Now it's only me
Remembering that smile
That I fell in love with
Lips so soft
Couldn't wait to kiss them
Rushing home to see you
To be together was everything
The center of my universe
I loved you so much
Hurt is what I gave
Too the woman I loved
Sorry for everything I did
Mistakes are apart of life
But now I know
What I lost
Until the day I die
You will always be the love of my life

The Past

Out of a water fountain
Is where you saw me drinking
With my roller blades on my feet
The skate park was a great time
That was the first place we met
A day to remember forever
After that day I wanted to be
With you and only you
Walks down the path
To my mother's house
Laying in my room for hours
Not letting go of you
When you went home
Calling me on the phone
Right away
Talking for hours
Unsperable
Is what we were
Spending every minute, hour and day
Coming to see me in the morning
Always before school
Writing me poems from the heart
I had yours and you had mine
Those were the moments
Time took them away from us
My heart holds those memories everyday
Why did I have to break your heart
Because you took care of mine
Can't believe I made bad choices
Regrets within
Dwelling on the past
Love came back in my life
But it's not the same
Please know my heart will always be yours

Scared

Being so scared of you
Running away
Avoiding it
Don't want to fall in love again
Afraid of being hurt
Make me happy, so I can do the same
Alone at the moment
Dates come and go
No more relationships
They get to complicated
Lets leave it simple
My life needs to be rebuilt
From my previous experiences
Give it time
Maybe I'll come around one day
Until then I will stay scared
Of that four letter word, Love

Finally over

Don't let it get you down
Stop thinking about them
No matter what they say
Keep your head up
Words don't hurt
They won't kill
Be strong
Walk on the right path
Everything will work out at the end
So many things can happen
Days will be good
Some maybe bad
Time will take the pain away
When everything gone
You will be glad
It is finally over

True

Coming into my life
Didn't even have a clue
That you were going to be there
Only seventeen years old
Thinking we knew what love was
Getting mad for little things
Insacure about each other
Jealousy always around
We couldn't keep peace unless we made love
What was wrong with this picture
Each day had to be spent together
Was it true love
Why did I question it
I just wanted to know if what we had was true

About You

How long will it take
Who will it be
Do I let them fall
Where do I meet you
What to say
These questions I ask about you
Will I let someone love me again
Should I give them the time of day
Why trust again
Could my heart be broken again
Would this be the biggest choice I have to make
These questions I ask about you

Who Really Loved Me

Who really loved me
You told me you loved me
Who really loved me
You bought me gifts
Who really loved me
You cooked dinner for me
Who really loved me
You cried when you missed me
Who really loved me
You were there to make me feel better
Who really loved me
You took all the pain away
Who really loved me
You were so sweet to me
Who really loved me
You said the most beautiful words to me
Who really loved me
You convinced me I was the only one
Who really loved me
With all the lies I can tell you never really loved me

I love you

I love you
When I go to sleep
I love you
When I wake up in the morning
I love you
When you have your sweats on
I love you
When you don't have makeup on
I love you
When your feeling down
I love you
When your feeling happy
I love you
When we fight
I love you
When we get married
I love you
When I pass away

Imagine

Imagine falling down
Imagine no one catching you
Imagine being alone
Imagine no light
Imagine nothing but darkness
Imagine the depression
Imagine never ending tears
Imagine a constant frown
Imagine yourself in my shoes

With or Without

A heart with no blood
Relationships without love
Rivers with no water
The sky without clouds
Movies with no actors
Nighttime without stars
Life with no old age
Minds without thoughts
Music with no beats
Songs without notes
Sleeping with no dreams
Hurt without pain
Clouds with no rain
Darkness without fear

Never coming back

You never took me back
I can understand
Cheated on you
Was the worse thing I ever did
Come back is what I want
But I know it's not going to happen
Please come back
So lonely without you
You are my only love
Make changes
Is what I'll do
Made promises
But you never came back
Hold on to this regret is what I'll do

Don't Deserve Too Be Loved

Layed down last night
Closed my eyes
Finally went to sleep
It took sometime
But it was worth it
My dream started
It was just us
You kissed me on the lips
Couldn't believe it
Such a beautiful woman
Was with me
Since I grew up so poor
And not like you
Feeling like I don't deserve
Too be loved
By someone like you
So now the sun has come up
Shines through my window
Waking up wishing
That I would have that same dream
Over and over every night

But You

Told you how I felt
But you just threw it in my face
Told you secrets
But you just threw it in my face
Told you things I would never tell anyone
But you just threw it in my face
Told you how I really felt about someone
But you just threw it in my face
Told you who I use too have a crush on
But you just threw it in my face
Told you my whole life story
But you just threw it in my face
Why did you ask all those questions
If you were just going too turn around
And throw it my face

Will you be there

If I hurt will you be there
If I cry will you be there
If I tell you how I feel will you be there
If I tell you my past will you be there
If I tell you all my problems will you be there
If I hurt I do something too you will you be there
If I open my heart too you will you be there
If I tell you how old I am will you be there
If I tell you my childhood will you be there
If I show you my lyrics will you be there
If I tell you what I want to do will you be there
If I walk away will you be there
These questions I ask
The person waiting for me
Will you really be there at the end

Come Back

Miss you so much
Since you left
Please come back
Listen to my problems
Drink with me one more time
Talk about what hurts
Walk in the door again
But I know you can't
You went somewhere good
Keep you in my dreams
Pray for you
Watch over me from the sky
Can't believe you left
Tell god I am a good person
Done so much bad
But my heart is good
I'll be there soon
Don't know what exact time
Hopefully soon because life isn't well
Moving away will not cure
What is waiting
I miss you so much
One day soon I will walk the sky
With both of you

Inside

Keep my feelings inside.
Bottled inside so no one can see. What really hurts.
Nights I can't sleep.
To much on my mind.
Money.
Family and friends.
Can't take it any more.
Don't want to face my problems.
Mad at myself for the people I hurt.
I'm sorry.
For everything I did.
I love you too death.
But I deal with the regret everyday.
Leaving isn't the answer.
I know you will cry when I do.
So I'm stuck here.
Thinking about the pain I caused.
Staying here for my family.
Your memories will always be in my mind.
The love for you will stay in my heart.
And the tears I cry will dry up.
But I'm still keeping everything inside.

The face

The sky
The starts
The clouds
The sun
The rain
The darkness
The sunshine
Look at me
My eyes
See my hate
Towards you
Hurting me
Is the worse
Thing that you ever did
I hate you
Never coming back
Is the slap in the face
That I give you back

What you did

You promised me the world
But I didn't get it
How could you lie
After everything
Gave you my heart
You broke it
So now
Don't trust women
You gave them a bad name
By just one person
Doing that
Lost my faith in people
You did it
No one else
Are you proud
Of what you did
If not
That's good
Losing the best thing
Is what you did
And I despise
Regret what happen
You're knocking on my front door
But I will not answer

But you can't

Let these tears fall
Trying too catch them
But you can't
Falling so fast
You can't stop nothing
Try too make me feel better
But you can't
So what can you do
Nothing
Because the hands of time
Have already been written
Can't do anything
Just seeing my future
Going down the drain
Please help me
So lonely
Come back
So it can be like before
Miss you so much

Sky

The sky is blue
And it's falling on me
With the rain drops
Clouds are so dark
No sunshine
Only nightfall
So dark
I can't see anything
Feeling so lost
And confused
Trying to find
The pieces of the puzzle
But I can't
Put it together
With missing pieces

Take us

Met you on a beautiful day
How could I forget
Waiting for your friends too come back
Standing all alone
Finally I saw the best smile
I had ever seen before
Brushing your hair back
Then you turned and looked at me
My heart stopped a beat
Looking at your brown eyes
Knowing you were one of a kind
From only one time of seeing you
How can a man feel this way
Turning your head away
Too give someone else attention
My heart starts too beat again
But this time it's faster
Wanting too go and speak to you
Afraid of the rejection
That I usually get
How else am I suppose to feel
When it happens
Finally get the courage
Walking with sweaty palms
Getting closer too you
Locking with each others eyes
Then I said hello
A butterfly came out
Talking for hours
Getting to know each other
Glad to spend the time
With someone so special
Only time will tell
Where this will take us

Complete

Words can only say so much
Actions say a lot more
When I tell you I love you
I mean it with all my heart
Being blessed with you in my life
Is the best thing that happened to me
Wishing we could of met earlier
But I finally found you
And my heart is complete

Sometimes

Sometimes I am afraid of success
Sometimes I am afraid too be alone
Sometimes I am afraid of the dark
Sometimes I am afraid to swim
Sometimes I am afraid to take the next step
Sometimes I am afraid to reach out
Sometimes I am afraid to learn
Sometimes I am afraid open my eyes
Sometimes I am afraid of life
Sometimes I am afraid of death
Sometimes I am afraid to cry in front of you
Sometimes I am afraid of falling
Sometimes I am afraid being on top
Sometimes I am afraid of letting you down
Sometimes I am just afraid of success

What I am

Keep my head down
So you can't see my face
My sorrow I keep
All to myself
Wipe the tears away
So you can't see them
Just another person walking by
Is what I am

So called

Friends will always be there
They will catch you
Open your heart
And they will listen
Ride shotgun on this ride
Life is what it's called
So loyal to you
Until you hurt them
Trust will not be there
Hurting everyday
For what a so-called friend did
A millions sorries will not fix it
I don't deserve to have you as a friend
But always remember
You were my best friend
Gave me food and shelter
Thank you so much
For everything you did

The bridge

Sleeping under the bridge
Use this piece of cardboard
As a mattress
With a pillow made of clothes
A cold night
With so much light
Coming from the moon and stars
Fingers are getting cold fast
When my body gets so numb
Cars drive by
People throw things at me
Counting the loose change
Thinking what it could buy me
Maybe I'll walk to the store in the morning
Look at my watch
The sun will rise soon
But I will stay under my bridge and sleep

Maybe one day

Mom left you on a dark night
Walking the streets with three kids
Plus one kid that was in your stomach
How will we sleep and eat
Is what the brother
Askes his mother
We have to go
Somewhere better
At the door steps
Of grandmothers house
Can we stay for the night
Morning comes
And daddy isn't there anymore
Mother is crying so much
I'm looking around
Smell fresh tortillas and eggs
They cooked the best breakfast
I was too young to understand
But now I am a grown man
Mother I understand why you left now
Love you until the end of time
Thank you for everything you do
Tell me I am doing wrong
Quit drinking so much
But how am I suppose to numb the pain
Trying to run away from it
It will keeps fallowing me everywhere
Why couldn't we be a family like on TV
Happiness looked so good
Sitting in this room alone
Thinking about what you did for us
Worked two jobs just too put food
On this little table

Why do times have to be so rough
Everything happens for a reason
Life has too stomp on me time over time
Family will always there for you
Hopefully all the pain will fade away
And maybe one day I will be happy

End Of Time

I love you
Kiss my lips
Let's hold hands
Tell me I am your everything
Close my eyes and still see the face
Of an angel
You are so beautiful to me
Don't care what anyone else says
Hold you close to me
Promise you will love me forever
Because I will
Even when I pass away
You will still be mine until the end of time

Anymore

Push you away
You can't stay
Were getting to close
All I need is a dose
Of you
This is true
Can't show my feelings
Tired of dealing
With everything inside
Acting blind
About what is in front of my face
Please leave my place
Staying alone
Don't call my phone
Trust no one anymore
Cause I can't give love anymore

Too Hear

I'll just hold you
All night
Hug me back
When you look
Into my eyes
You'll get lost
Like you have never been
Just tell him you love me
And I will tell you I love you back
Kiss me
With your beautiful lips
Taste my love
That money can't buy
Missing you everyday
When I lay down at night
I think about you
Hurts so bad I can't be with you
Please hold me in your heart
One day I will come back
When the rain drys up
You will be there to catch my tears
No on else can feel my pain
But you will take the time
To hear what really happened in my life